Purple Ink
A Childhood in Tanka

poems by

Carole Johnston

Finishing Line Press
Georgetown, Kentucky

Purple Ink
A Childhood in Tanka

ACKNOWLEDGMENTS

Several of these poems have been published in the following journals.
Atlas Poetica—Journal of World Tanka
Bright Stars—An Organic Tanka Anthology
Best of Five Line Poems
Cattails—Collected Works of United Haiku and Tanka Society
Moonbathing—Journal of Women's Tanka
Red Lights—Tanka Journal
Skylark—Tanka Journal
Undertow—Tanka Journal

Publisher: Leah Maines

Editor: Christen Kincaid

Cover Art: Cover art was created by Amber Johnston from a photo by Carole
Johnston, shot at the Living Arts And Science Center in Lexington, Kentucky.

Author Photo: Amber Johnston

Cover Design: Elizabeth Maines McCleavy

Printed in the USA on acid-free paper.
Order online: www.finishinglinepress.com
            also available on amazon.com

Author inquiries and mail orders:
Finishing Line Press
P. O. Box 1626
Georgetown, Kentucky 40324
U. S. A.

Table of Contents

Dedication

Forward and quote from Matthew Dickman

neon deep 1

white box houses 2

Cleremont Avenue / where nothing............................ 3

Cleremont Avenue / enveloped 4

we play in the attic 5

scratchy—the warp.. 6

one night.. 7

I sit crosslegged... 8

before we.. 9

nose pressed 10

first summer 11

I wear a scarf 12

little girls 13

Joannie 14

tiny girls... 15

even... 16

those girls... 17

drinking tea 18

Grandpop 19

Uncle Roy 20

the day I slather... 21

that salesman... 22

now I am 23

Merlin.. 24

Morgan Le Fay 25

kids don't care / when I leap...................................... 26

kids don't wait / five steps 27

one summer day 28

Victor Polumbo.. 29

snake dream 30

Grandpop takes me 31

I run wild 32

sometimes I am.. 33

kindergarten.. 34

I dance.. 35

Mother sings.. 36

every night..37
sent away...38
older sister 39
fairy tale books..40
green elixir...41
pink and white 42
I play alone 43
 kids don't want 44
seven years old 45
crayons...46
second grade 47
in third grade 48
kicked out of...49
black ink..50
miracle 51
I shock..52
in my room..53
from my window 54
lost in a book...55
late for school...56
kids tattle on me 57
teacher's voice...58
soft dead bunnies..59
Mother sends me 60
my slow summers..61
diary pages..62
now kids call me 63
the first time..64
one night..65
in the stocking...66
Daddy and I...67
model trains streaked..68
one Christmas..69
childhood daydream / I slash......................................70
childhood daydream / I jump 71
those fireflies 72
I believe..73
I climb the peach tree..74
my dog and I 75
sometimes / I play...76
I am that girl..77

new girl moves 78
that younger girl 79
new girl who lives..80
sometimes I wonder...81
so... I say, "Hi" 82
we don't know 83
ten years old 84
Mother warns me 85
is it absinthe?..86
some nights 87
Cleremont Avenue / nothing 88
 gingerbread house 89
we ignore her...90
ordinary 91
hopscotch...92
BIO

In memory of Kathy Ziegler.

Gratitude to Bill Johnstone who helped me find her grave and untangle a forty five year old mystery.

Gratitude to Dr. Jonel Sallee for continuing moral support.

from *Lents District* by Mathew Dickman

"…Dear 82nd avenue, dear 92nd and Foster,
I am your strange son,
you saved me when I needed saving
and I remember your arms wrapped around
my bassinet like patrol cars wrapped around
the school yard
the night Jason went crazy—
waving his father's gun above his head,
bathed in red and blue flashing lights,
all American, broken in half and beautiful."

"Lents District" gives me chills every time I read it.

My old neighborhood was dull compared to Lents. Disgruntled to be "*from*" such an ordinary place, I remembered that something did happen on Cleremont Avenue, a few years after I left, and that event was rooted in **my** past as much as anyone's. Inspired by Mathew Dickman's remarkable poem, I began writing one tanka after another, about my childhood, from age 3 through age 10, juxtaposing dark and light. These poems may seem sad, but I see them as the chronicle of an odd child growing **strong** in spite of never being "neurotypical." I was "saved" by fantasy. Perhaps it is a story for all poets.

neon deep
memories of childhood
dream shrouded
startled by huge dark wings
my pen dipped in purple ink

white box houses
row on row of square blocks
street after street
chalk on the sidewalks
walk-to-school kids

Cleremont Avenue
where nothing ever happens
under maple trees
my father plants roses
magnolias and irises

summer day
glitters with green beetles
I pluck them
drop them in a glass jar
watch them sunsparkle

Cleremont Avenue
enveloped in tree cloud
wrapped in tacky boredom
one house like a castle
across the concrete street

we play in the attic
of the gingerbread castle
hiding in closets
never knowing where
the crooked man lurks

scratchy—the warp
of that rose covered rug
on my knees
watching my child reflection
dark in the glass door

twirling
on the flowery carpet
until
I collapse dizzy
the ceiling spins above me

one night
I am three years old
a magic carpet
sweeps me from my crib
carries me on dark journeys

I sit crosslegged
on that little carpet
flying around
the midnight house
Queen of Shadows

before we
ever learn about sin
we steal
a bunch of marigolds
sell them on the street

rolling in green
grass down the front lawn
my head spins
sky whirls above me
I jump up and roll again

nose pressed
into purple irises
tall as I am
inhaling sweetness
among the angry bees

I play alone
on the back porch pretend
I'm a doctor
healing iridescent green
bugs tiny feet scratch my hands

first summer
vacation bible school
chirping songs
my child mind imagines
Jesus is a fat woman

"lavender's blue"
I sing a song to the trees
tumbling
green in dandelions
sprite summer day

I wear a scarf
tie-dyed at summer day camp
blood red
sky blue and purple
Lisa's mom laughs at my art

little girls
dainty as garden birds
with tea sets
I wonder why sometimes
they won't let me play

paper boats
and mud puddles
earth worms
wiggle on sidewalks
spring rain

Joanie
a tiny blackbird
Lisa
a chirping sparrow
Fiona a bossy pigeon

tiny girls
pretend to drink pretend tea
from pink plastic
pretend tea pots extending
pinky fingers in the air

sometimes
I write little songs
about pickles
I sing them in my head
while meandering to school

even my
new red Keds
do not
make those girls like me
shoe laces always untied

those girls
in their frilly white dresses
flowers in hair
they will crown Mother Mary
I offer Daddy's roses

Daddy
teaches me to plant
a rose bush
digs deep into dark soil
squiggly worms glowing

drinking tea
with Edwardian great aunts
other kids
learn to skate and ride bikes
I learn about guilt

Aunt Lottie
has crocheted a warm afghan
just for me
red and black granny squares
because I have no grandma

Grandpop
chews tobacco
spits it
into an old tin can
takes me to the movies

Uncle Roy
has sandpaper whiskers
scratches my face
with his big moon jaws
his ugly bigoted words

I ride
the painted pony
reaching
for the sparkly gold ring
sister watches me go round

the day I slather
myself with mud to see
how I would look
if born with brown skin
Mother hoses me down fast

I sneak
out at night and stare
at the moon
blooming with roses
along the stone wall

that salesman
who flimflammed my mother
into buying
all those fairy tale books
he saved my life

now I am
the neighborhood witch
lashed to a tree
transmogrified from
evil to good and back

Merlin
stars shimmering on
his indigo robe
I love the runic picture
in that antique book

Morgan Le Fay
hair streaming down her back
spell book
and a knife in her hands
black eyes glitter from the page

kids don't care
when I leap into
the pool
shouting, "I am the famous
flying Robin Hood Dog"

lucky stones
under the lilac tree
gold pebbles
like sunflowers where I
dig a hole to China

kids don't wait
five steps ahead of me
on bikes
roller skates double dutch
I crash and skin my knees

chocolate ice cream cone
drips down my arms and legs
freezes my face
babysitter holds my hand
all the long walk home

one summer day
I talk some kids into
playing "giants"
jumping in piles of grass
smelling of chlorophyl

sometimes
we are horses prancing
around
the playground whinnying
at kids and teachers too

Victor Polumbo
hides matches in his shoes
brags about burning
a whole vacant lot
he smokes through my dreams

mother warns
don't stare at the sun
but sometimes
I can't resist the
spectacle of rainbows

snake dream
filled with orange poison
abandoned
my parents in a plane
Victor Polumbo wins

Grandpop takes me
on the bus to the movies
buys me candy
sunk in dark velvet seats—blood
red space creatures—my eyes pop

I run wild
in the cemetery
playing
with my ghost friends
Mother calls me "morbid"

my friend Silva
lives in the graveyard
under an old tree
sometimes I go and sit there
talk to her sing her a song

sometimes I am
a noisy child bellowing
like a dragon
shrieking like a witch
before they shut me up

Aunt dot says
"Why do kids draw those colors
around the sun?"
why can't she see the lines
through my rainbow eyes?

kindergarten
I fail shoe tying
time telling
excel at paper eating
paste tastes like mint

begging
for a dog I weep
all night
soon a white puppy with
black spots appears

I dance
with the big rag doll
my mother
singing in the kitchen
never sees me rock

mother's arms
so strong mashing apples
in the colander
she boils them for sauce
our house full of sweetness

Mother sings
along with big band radio
her whirring voice
I swing and sway with
the *Make Believe Ballroom*

every night
my sister reads poems to me
five years old
imagination soaring
over sea and stars

sent away
before the wedding
a nuisance
getting in the way is
my role in the family

bees swarm
sweet rotting apples
beneath the tree
my autumn chore is
scooping up the windfalls

older sister married
who used to read poems
at bedtime from
watercolor books about
sugar plum trees and fairies

fairy tale books
pages scattered with magic
on Mother's lap
I wait for the words but
she "rests her eyes" then sleeps

green elixir
Mother's "nerve medicine"
in a bottle
on the top kitchen shelf
is it really my fault?

jumping waves
goosebumps on my skin
holding hands
safe with Mom and Daddy
hot sun cold green ocean

pink and white
organdy pinafores hang
in my closet
I don't want to look
like a porcelain doll

I ride
kid sized swan boats
parents wave
as I circle round
white wooden wings

I play alone
in my lavender room
gazing at books
I still can't read
about elves and fairies

after grandpop
dies and goes to heaven
I get a new room
in the azure/purple attic
share a window with the moon

kids don't want
to study the maps
of fairyland
I draw them at school
instead of doing math

swooping
down the slide
my dog
friend follows me
everywhere

seven years old
I sing in the children's choir
thanksgiving songs
...when morning is breaking...
words burn into memory

crayons
are magic wands
colors
from my neon mind
flow in suns and moons

crayons
my favorite things
they smell
like bees and flowers
like comets in the night sky

second grade
I fail everything
still can't read
colored chalk rainbows
save me from sadness

Mary and I
draw chalk horses on the board
teacher makes us
wash our magic off each day
colors swirl in the bucket

in third grade
kids play "Davey Crocket"
with "coonskin" caps
I play fairies and dragons
wild wings on the swing

kicked out of
the third grade musical
too clumsy to dance
that new turquoise dress
hanging in the closet

my desk
cluttered with crayons
scissors
glitter and glue
no room for math books

inside my desk
I keep safety pins
stick them
through the calluses
on my fingers

under the table
I become a secret spy
listening
Tuesday grown-up gossip
Mother's canasta club

black ink
sharp on white pages
words hop
about back and forth
I force them to stand still

miracle
sister gone ...soothing myself
with books
my brain makes words stand still
now I have power

I shock
the third grade teacher
her scowling face
now I'm the best reader
in her precious class

in my room
a window seat for reading
and moon gazing
watching in furtive silence
the lonely dome of night

from my window
I stare at the owly moon
and the street lamp
that stands on the corner
scribble in my diary

lost in a book
behind the rhododendrons
on the front porch
those wicked neighbor girls
roll their eyes at me

exploring
the school library I find
"Silver Pennies"
a book of fairy poems
fine thick paper deep cut words

late for school
sailing paper boats
in puddles
I find a dead bunny
stuff it in my book bag

kids
tattle on me
because
the soft dead bunny
is safe inside my desk

teacher's voice
like a scratchy record
"get that thing
out of this room" so I
stash it in my locker

soft dead bunnies
not allowed in lockers
I creep outside
hide it in a pile of leaves
sing a strange church song

mother sends me
to the movies alone
nine years old
I ride the city bus
monsters do not scare me

on the boardwalk
my first hot crinkle cut fry
frozen custard
sticky saltwater taffy
waves crash in the night

my slow summers
reading poems
in a hammock
watching clouds wander
through peach branches

I climb
up the apple boughs
reaching for
blueluminous sky
scraped by dappled bark

diary pages
written by flashlight
in the dark
I read the burning words
Anne Frank wrote long ago

I wonder why
teachers like smart kids so much
but in sixth grade
I'm a smart kid too—reading
Ivanhoe instead of math

teacher asks "Who
knows what the druids were?"
my mind sees
images of hooded men
I raise my hand—I'm right

now kids call me
the "walking dictionary"
always reading
traveling to worlds
they can't even dream

the first time
my mother tells me
"fix it yourself"
I put a band-aid on
my own skinned knee

in sixth grade
I write a story of my
dog's first snow
her white paws freezing
teacher reads it to the class

one night
the devil visits me
huge black wings
unfurled and I scream...
"just a dream," Mother says

in the stocking
every year an orange
gingerbread
Santa cookie the scent
of citrus and spice

Daddy and I
draping silver tinsel
on the tree
one strand at at time
twinkles in his eyes

model trains streaked
steely through the tunnel
around the village
handmade by Grandpop
Daddy and Uncle Dave

one Christmas
a silver music box
plays *Stardust*
I spin and swirl
dip and twirl

that winter night
riding in the back seat
I hear bells
ringing snow songs
my parents hear nothing

childhood daydream...
I slash the window screen
sharp kitchen knife
stabbing at the air
outside in the bushes

childhood daydream...
I jump across church pews
shouting I hate you
singing *Old Rugged Cross*
no one can catch me

those fireflies
we love to catch and smear
their glow
on our faces like
luminous warpaint

I believe
there are fairies
in the boxwood
my fantasy destroyed...
by that black hearted old man

I climb the peach tree
Grandpop planted in our yard
shoe laces tangled
crash down and climb again
knees bruised and bloody

my dog and I
explore the cemetery
new red Keds
tramp between tomb stones
deep in mud and flowers

sometimes
I play in mud with
the boys
blond haired bully hurls sticks
at my dog as we race home

makes no sense
playing with boys
they dump me
into a cardboard box
filled with earth worms

I am that girl
skipping barefoot in the rain
splashing
through mud puddles
Mother's friends gossip in awe

new girl moves
into the gingerbread house
no more days
chasing ghosts in that attic
hiding from the crooked man

that younger girl
alone on her front porch
so much like me
I spy on her
never try to talk to her

new girl who lives
in the gingerbread house
unbrushed hair
plaid flannel shirts
she watches us—we watch her

the new girl's name
is Kathy who plays alone
on her front porch
what's the difference between
the two of us loners?

sometimes
I wonder why she never
speaks to
me or the other girls
her sad black eyes

so... I say,"Hi"
to that silent little girl
something like
fire flashes deep in her eyes
I scuttle home to read

larch trees brood on
the gingerbread castle
I cross the street
singing 'widdershins' like
a fairy tale I've read

we don't know
someday she'll crack and fall
like broken bones
˙we play—we go to school
we don't know the crooked man

fairy tale prince
rescued his sister
from an evil
wizard "widdershins open
the dark tower tonight"

ten years old
I begin to hide away
from laughter
crowds make my head ache
touch makes me shudder

Mother warns me
don't go near the woods
I walk the dog
darker than darkness
between the trees

I never
thought that broody girl
needed
to be rescued where dark trees
always infused me with light

is it absinthe
that green glass bottle
on the top shelf
does it swing my mother
in the belly of the sea?

little girls
ten year old mermaids
swirl the waves
seaweed in our hair
washed by salt and sun

some nights
the moon bleeds silver
keeps me awake
trying to write the future
who will little girls become?

Cleremont Avenue
nothing ever happens
so many little girls
live in different worlds
on the same street

gingerbread house
surrounded by larch trees
inhabited
by that lonely girl
who *set herself on fire*

we ignore her
as if we know a secret
that someday
blue lights and sirens will scream
down Cleremont to that girl's door

ordinary
Cleremont Avenue
silent street
no one knows our secrets
hearts we never share

hopscotch
and jump rope rhymes
sung in
a minor key written
in chalk and purple ink

Carole Johnston remembers her childhood as an impressionistic film. She is dedicated to learning the art of writing tanka in the Japanese tradition and spends most of her time lost in "haiku moments." Living and writing in Lexington, Kentucky, she finds time for the mind to wander. Her two other books of poems are, *Journeys: Getting Lost*—Finishing Line Press and *Manic Dawn*—Wildflower Poetry Press.